James Barr Roberston

The Confederate Debt and Private Southern Debts

James Barr Roberston

The Confederate Debt and Private Southern Debts

ISBN/EAN: 9783337004453

Printed in Europe, USA, Canada, Australia, Japan

Cover: Foto ©ninafisch / pixelio.de

More available books at **www.hansebooks.com**

THE CONFEDERATE DEBT

AND

PRIVATE SOUTHERN DEBTS.

BY

J. BARR ROBERTSON.

LONDON:
WATERLOW AND SONS Limited, 95 & 96, LONDON WALL
1884.

PRICE ONE SHILLING.

CONTENTS.

	PAGE
I. Introduction	1
II. The Confederate States in relation to Foreign States	2
III. The Confederate States in relation to the United States	4
IV. The Dollar Bonds	6
V. The Sterling Cotton Bonds	8
VI. The Fourteenth Amendment	15
VII. The Opinions of six Continental Jurists	18
VIII. Cases quoted in favour of the Claims of the Bondholders	24
IX. The Equities in the Original Controversy between North and South reserved	29
X. An Omitted Claim against the United States	32

NOTE.

Although the following observations were not written for the public, it has nevertheless been thought that the subject is one of sufficient importance, both in the United States and Europe, to warrant publication. These views are offered, therefore, in the hope that public and unprejudiced discussion on both sides of the Atlantic may enable some settlement to be arrived at by the United States of the just and legitimate claims that are set forth in the following pages.

J. B. R.

THE CONFEDERATE DEBT

AND

PRIVATE SOUTHERN DEBTS.

I.—INTRODUCTION.

I HAVE been asked by several large holders of Confederate Bonds both Americans and Englishmen, to give an opinion on the practical aspects of the Confederate Debt, and for this purpose copies have been placed in my hands of "the Case" of the Bondholders, the opinions of six Continental Jurists, and several pamphlets bearing on the subject and on the proceedings that have been taken by the Bondholders. I have no pretensions whatever to be a lawyer, and therefore the following observations must be regarded as simply and solely those of a financier and a man of business.

The conclusions arrived at in the following pages are,—that the Confederate States had only belligerent and not international rights; that the Confederacy being an illegal corporation according to United States law could not issue Bonds which would be valid against either the United States or the legal State Governments of the South; that therefore neither the Cotton Bonds nor the Dollar Bonds have any validity whatever as Confederate Debt in the absence of the Confederacy; that there is nothing in the opinions and cases adduced in support of the Bonds which really conflicts with this view of their illegality in the United States; that the equities arising out of the original controversy between North and South, not being cognizable by any Court, are reserved as subject matter for consideration by the United States, and are therefore outside the scope of the present discussion;

and that there is in the Dollar Bonds an omitted international claim against the United States for payment of private debts owed by Southern citizens to Europeans at the beginning of the war, and which are now represented by Dollar Bonds that were sent to them as the only means of remittance from the Southern States, and that these debts, and the claims of Southern citizens not engaged in the war, and of Europeans, for property taken by force and for which Confederate Bonds were compulsorily tendered, are not in any way affected by the Fourteenth Amendment, and therefore ought to be paid by the United States.

II.—THE CONFEDERATE STATES IN RELATION TO FOREIGN STATES.

In consequence of the hostile action taken by the Confederate States against the United States, the blockade of the Southern ports was instituted on 19th April, 1861, and on 13th May the British Government issued a Proclamation of Neutrality in which the Confederate States were recognised as belligerents. This recognition as belligerents was inevitable as soon as the United States declared their intention of establishing a blockade, not with the view of Foreign Powers deciding anything as between the belligerents themselves, but as declaring that a state of hostilities had arisen of which it was essential that the citizens of neutral nations should be informed, and that the conduct to be observed by them and the risks to which they would be liable, might be duly made known on the authority of their respective Governments. The Confederate States, it must be observed, were simply provinces in rebellion against the lawfully constituted authority of the United States, and had none of the international status of an independent nation. If they had been an independent power at war with another independent power, their status would have been totally different from what it could possibly be as belligerents without the previous condition of independence. So far, therefore, as the British and other Foreign Governments had a positive duty to perform, it was to protect the interests of their own citizens by recognising the Confederates as belligerents and by giving warning that trade with the ports of the Confederate States was suspended, and that vessels attempting to enter or leave these ports were liable to seizure and the ships and cargoes to confiscation. The recognition as belligerents was an act of immediate necessity in consequence of the declaration of blockade, but the strenuous attempts of the Confederate States to obtain from the European Powers their recognition as an independent state, entirely failed. If the European Powers had recognised their independence while war was still going on, and the ultimate issue still undecided, this recognition would not have been of any benefit to the Bondholders, as the fact that the Confederate States had never been independent of the United States, and did not become so, would have justified the United States in complaining that the European Powers had done them a grievous wrong in recognising as existing in the Confederate States an independent status which, at the time of recognition, did not exist, and as a matter of fact did not afterwards come into existence.

In the absence therefore in the Confederate States of the previous status of an independent nation, the Foreign Powers, by taking the necessary steps to recognise them as belligerents, assumed an attitude solely of expectancy. War had arisen not between two independent members of the family of nations, but in the bosom of a single nation, and although it was imperative to issue proclamations of neutrality to define rights and obligations as affecting neutrals and belligerents, yet it was the duty of the powers in friendly relations with the United States to wait for the issue of the hostilities, and not to recognise the Confederate States as an independent member of the family of nations until they should have established their independence. As a matter of fact, they failed to establish their independence, and with that failure their position as belligerents and their hopes of becoming a separate Republic came to an end. Thus they never reached that position of independence in which they would have acquired an international status, and therefore in their defeat they had no international claim to consideration, nor had the United States or Foreign Powers any international duty to perform towards them, nor could their treatment become an international question, seeing that the United States alone, and not the Confederate States, were represented in the family of nations. The British Government had therefore no grounds for offering even friendly advice to the United States as to the treatment of the Confederates when the civil war came to an end, and the authority of the United States was re-established over the territory temporarily held by the Confederate Government.

[20201]

III.—THE CONFEDERATE STATES IN RELATION TO THE UNITED STATES.

The States that composed the Confederacy had been States of the United States with certain rights, duties and disabilities defined in the Constitution and laws of the United States. The Constitution provided no means by which a State could legally withdraw from the Union, nor any method by which a State could supersede the tribunals and authority of the United States, enter into a confederacy with other States, and maintain a government independent of and in hostility to the United States, except by a policy of violence to the law and the Constitution. When, therefore, the Southern States seceded and entered into a Confederacy with a view to establishing themselves as an independent republic, they deliberately and intentionally violated the Constitution of the United States. It is not intended to discuss here the question whether they were justified on grounds of equity in acting as they did, or what were the merits of the sectional controversy between North and South, as these grounds of equity are political and not international. The question before the Bondholders is, what are the practical issues involved in the case of the Bondholders on which they may found a valid claim to complete or partial payment?

The Southern States had the most complete liberty to appeal to the "sacred right of insurrection," and they did so; but the Northern States had also the fullest claim to appeal to the "sacred right of suppressing insurrection," and they did so. It was open to the United States to have permitted this violation of the Constitution, and to have allowed the Confederate States to establish their separate republic in peace. They did not, however, elect to adopt this course, and in their determination to vindicate the law and the Constitution, there is but little cause for surprise, because independent nations cannot permit bodies of their own citizens to separate themselves and to set up as independent nations without making a resolute effort to maintain the national territory in its integrity. The United States, following what is regarded as the universal duty of nations in such circumstances, determined to attempt the suppression of the rebellion as the only means of national self-preservation.

This determination, it must be observed, was not to attempt the conquest of the whole or of any portion of an independent country with which some difficulty might have arisen. The United States had been deprived of their lawful jurisdiction over the Southern States by the forcible suppression of their courts and of their authority, and illegal and usurping State Governments had displaced the legal State Governments, and had formed themselves into an illegal confederacy for the purpose of preventing the United States from exercising their lawful and constitutional authority within the so-called Confederate States. Thus the duty which the United States undertook was to re-establish their lawful authority, and as the Confederate States resisted by force all attempts to reimpose this authority, the United States were compelled to resort to hostilities for the purpose of re-establishing their lawful jurisdiction. The Confederate States had therefore no warrant in the Constitution of the United States for their secession and compact, and thus the act of secession was practically an appeal by them to the arbitrament of the sword, in the expectation that the tribunal of war would decide in favour of their claim to separate national independence, and against the claim of the United States to have their legal authority re-established.

There the question rested from February, 1861, till April, 1865, when the tribunal of war gave its decision in favour of the re-establishment of the jurisdiction of the United States. The appeal by the Southern States to the "sacred right of insurrection" had failed, while the appeal by the United States to the "sacred right of suppressing insurrection" was successful. Now it must be particularly observed that the United States added not a square mile of territory nor a single new citizen as the result of the four years' war. They simply re-established at tremendous cost that jurisdiction over certain States of the Union which had been for a time suspended in consequence of the unlawful acts of usurping State Governments and a usurping Confederacy. By once more coming under the jurisdiction of the Courts of the United States, the acts of the State Governments and of the Confederacy had to be dealt with by the Constitution and laws of the United States; and therefore it was inevitable that all acts performed directly or indirectly in pursuance of the war should be declared to be illegal acts.

Had the Confederate States established their independence, they would not have been amenable to any tribunals except those that they had themselves set up, and they would have shaped their legislation and their institutions to suit themselves. But as they failed in this, the United States not only re-established their former jurisdiction, but by virtue of their success in war, and the unconditional surrender of the enemy, they had the right of a conqueror to dictate the conditions on which they would treat the conquered, grant or refuse amnesty, impose political or other disabilities, confiscate property, imprison the leaders, or do any other act that might seem to them fit in the circumstances. As guardians of the Republic they had also imposed on them the duty of taking such precautions in the methods by which they permitted political reconstruction of the States, as to provide in the amplest manner for the security and integrity of the Union; while they were bound to provide by new legislation, or by additions to the Constitution, such stipulations as would as far as possible hinder and discourage all attempts at rebellion in the future.

IV.—THE DOLLAR BONDS.

Some observations may now be offered regarding the origin of the Dollar Bonds, that is, those Bonds which were issued by the Confederacy within the Confederate States, and the grounds on which it is alleged that they ought to be paid either by the United States or by the individual States that formerly composed the Confederacy. The first Dollar Bonds were issued on the 28th February, 1861, in exchange for cash, before the war broke out, and therefore before belligerent rights were conceded to the Confederate States. It is argued that this loan has an inferior claim to payment to those issued after war began, owing to the fact that the Confederate States were not then recognised as belligerents, because it is assumed that the recognition as belligerents conferred the power of raising loans. The subsequent Dollar Bonds were almost entirely issued in payment for property, services, &c., and as they were issued during the period when belligerent rights were recognised, it is alleged that they form a perfectly valid claim against the United States, and a stronger claim still against the individual States formerly in the Confederacy.

There does not seem, however, to be any difference between the Dollar Bonds of 28th February, 1861, and those subsequently issued, so far as the authority of the issuer or the legality of the issues is concerned. A very wide distinction might be drawn between Bonds accepted voluntarily for cash, and those issued practically by compulsion for property taken for the purposes of the Confederacy, because the former must rest entirely on the legal validity of the Bond, whereas holders of the latter may fairly claim an equitable consideration of the circumstances in which they were forcibly deprived of their property even if it was used for the purposes of the war. But the allegation which is so frequently put forward, that the recognition of the Confederate States as belligerents gave them a power of issuing loans which the United States, if ultimately the conquerors, would be, according to international law, bound to acknowledge and pay, seems to be entirely without foundation; though equitable claims may justly be made, arising, not out of the possession of Confederate Bonds, but out of the fact of numbers of individuals having been deprived of property by force, it being immaterial, except as evidence, whether Bonds were or were not given or taken for such property.

The distinction drawn between the Bonds issued for cash and those issued for property is of no importance so far as the right of the Confederacy to issue Bonds is concerned, seeing that both classes of Bonds were voluntarily issued by the same authority, namely, the Government of the Confederate States. When the British Government recognised the Confederates as belligerents, it did not expressly or impliedly confer any power of raising loans, which had a legal or international claim to be paid, whether the Confederacy succeeded or failed. At the outset of the struggle very large interests of British citizens were involved in the hostilities, and Great Britain recognised the condition of belligerency so as to be able to regulate those incidents in which its citizens were necessarily concerned. But the reason why the Dollar Bonds have no legal validity as Confederate Debt against either the United States or the present Southern States is, that under the Constitution of the United States there is no right in a State to secede, to enter into a compact with other States, or to carry on war against the United States; and, therefore, when in April, 1865, United States authority was re-establised, and United States tribunals restored in the territory formerly held by the Confederates, all those acts of the State

Governments and of the Confederacy which they performed as seceded States, or as a Confederacy of such, were, as was inevitable, declared illegal. In particular, the Confederacy as a new power, and one altogether unknown to the Constitution, could not possibly be regarded as having done one single legal act, although naturally much that it did in the four years had to be accepted by the United States on grounds of equity. Thus, when all the statutes and acts of the Confederacy were swept away, it came to pass that the acts authorising the issue of Bonds and their redemption, were of no avail whatever, and it became impossible to obtain before any United States Court a hearing in regard to the Bonds or the acts by which they were authorised. Not only according to the United States law were the Bonds issued for an illegal and improper purpose, but in view of the law by which they must be judged, the usurping State Governments and the Confederacy were illegal corporations. If, therefore, the Confederacy was illegal, all its acts were illegal; and as an illegal corporation, it could have no legal successor. It would seem, therefore, that all the Dollar Bonds, were, according to United States law, that is, according to the only law that can take cognisance of them, illegally issued by an illegal corporation unknown to the law and unauthorised by it, and as such have no legal validity whatever, as Confederate Debt, against the United States or the present State Governments of the South.

Neither the usurping State Governments nor the Confederacy ever had any independent international position which would have entitled them, in the eyes of other nations, to rights and to consideration as the defenders of their national existence. So that international law is dumb as to rights of defeated rebel States to have the debts incurred in trying to achieve their independence paid by the conqueror, or paid by levying taxes upon those States when once the conqueror's former jurisdiction is re-established.

V.—THE STERLING COTTON BONDS.

In the case of the Sterling Cotton Loan, it is alleged that that was a purely commercial transaction for value, and that, not being contraband, it could not, according to the law of nations, be declared invalid by the conqueror of the State that issued it, as he must take over the just obligations of the conquered State. Moreover, as the subscribers to this loan were neutrals, and not belligerents, their loan was not liable to confiscation on the ground of belligerency, as the Dollar Loans might possibly be. As an undoubted proof that the Cotton Loan was only a commercial transaction, it is shown that the bonds were convertible into cotton "at any time not later than six months after a ratification of a treaty of peace between the present belligerents." While it is alleged that this is a valid loan according to international law, it is somewhat strange that, if it be so, it has hitherto been impossible to acquire for it any international standing. And yet this must not be confounded with cases like Greece, Spain, and other defaulting countries, which, for a long time, simply ignored their debt, and made no provision for paying it. Those were valid debts according to international law, although settlement was long delayed. But the case of the Cotton Loan is entirely different. The holders of it claim that it is an international debt, and that payment is unjustly withheld. But it must be recollected that there have been international commissions sitting to examine into the claims arising out of the war with the South, and that the British Government has presented and urged those that possessed any validity. But the claims of the Cotton Bondholders have never reached any of those tribunals, although Great Britain has paid the Alabama Award, and the United States the Fishery Award. The reason why the Cotton Bondholders have failed in getting their claims brought before any international tribunal is that they are not international claims at all, the Confederate States never having had an international existence.

In favour of its validity, however, the Opinion of two eminent lawyers is quoted—namely, of the present Lord Cairns and the present Lord Justice Cotton, as it was given on the issue of the Cotton Loan in London, on 23rd February, 1863.

"We are of opinion that it will not be a violation of any law of this country, or of any principle of international law, to advertise the loan in this country as a loan to the Confederate States, upon bonds, the amount of which is payable by those States."

"We are of opinion that there is not any legal objection to the contractors offering the bonds for sale in England to the public at a price and on terms to be stated in a prospectus."

This opinion is entirely negative, and is merely an assertion that the advertising of the Cotton Loan would not be illegal. There can be no doubt that the question put before them for their opinion was all but practically worthless for the purpose of eliciting an authoritative statement as to the rights and responsibilities of subscribers. Now it is evident that there are at least four conditions of legality or illegality involved in the opinion of these two eminent lawyers that were very important to intending subscribers :—

(1.) The Cotton Loan might be perfectly legal in this country, and all subscriptions to it and dealings in it might be recognized by the Courts of this country, so far as the validity of contracts was concerned.

(2.) The Cotton Loan might not be illegal in this country, and yet British Courts might refuse to give effect to contracts in the bonds as contrary to public policy.

(3.) The Cotton Loan was legal in the Confederate States, as it is to be presumed it was issued under proper authority according to the laws of the Confederate States.

(4.) The Cotton Loan was entirely illegal in the United States.

These were the real issues in the Cotton Loan, and, as such, they ought to have been submitted for the opinion of counsel. At the time of the issuing of the loan, the Bondholders' rights were at least those stated in (2) and (3). It is all but perfectly certain that the loan had not the benefit of (1); but it is of little importance as to the validity of (1), (2) and (3), as the entire question now centres in (4), and the hope of the Bondholders is that this loan, which must have been declared by counsel to be illegal in the United States at the time it was issued, if an opinion had been asked for on that point, will nevertheless be paid by the United States, or by the Southern States acting with the permission of the United States.

The loan was perfectly legal in this country, in so far that no one subscribing to it was in any danger of personal consequences as the result of such subscription. The fact that the British Government did not prohibit it only showed that they did not regard it as an infringement of neutrality; but from this it cannot be inferred that the contracts of subscription would have been enforced by British Courts. It is in the highest degree probable that such contracts would not have been enforced by British Courts, although it might be no infringement of neutrality in the British Government to permit their citizens to take the loan if they were so minded. There was no illegality, according to British law, in paying money for the Bonds of the Confederate States, and this is the practical meaning of the opinion of Lord Cairns and Lord Justice Cotton quoted above. The Bonds, as issued, carried no disability with them, so there was no objection to their being held; and, as they were Bonds of the Confederate States, the opinion of these two lawyers was that they were valid Bonds as against those States. But they expressed no opinion whatever as to the recourse of the Bondholders against the United States if the Confederate States were defeated; and it is difficult to believe that they could have given any countenance to the idea that, failing the Confederate States, the United States would be liable for the repayment of the Cotton Bonds.

The stipulation that the Bonds could be converted into cotton " at any time not later than six months after a ratification of a peace between the present belligerents," shows that the promoters and subscribers of the loan regarded the issue of the conflict as certain to be in favour of the Confederates, and therefore never contemplated the possibility of what really happened, namely, that there would be no ratification of peace, but an unconditional surrender to the United States. There cannot be the slightest doubt that the terms of the loan would have been fulfilled to the letter, if, as the subscribers to the loan confidently expected, the Confederate States had been successful in establishing their independence. But as they failed in their efforts at independence, and never had any international recognition as an independent

State, the Cotton Loan has no international character whatever, and, therefore, its validity is a question for the United States Courts.

It is also asserted by some of the authorities in this case that the subscribers to the loan had no knowledge of the purpose to which the money was to be applied, and that therefore the Bonds were not liable to confiscation. When we consider the fact already referred to, that the Bonds were exchangeable for cotton at any time within six months after the ratification of peace, it can hardly be asserted that the subscribers to the loans were ignorant of the purpose to which it was to be applied. They subscribed for an option which depended on the contingency that a ratification of peace would take place. But, whatever importance might be attached, if it were an international question, to ignorance as to the objects to which the loan was to be applied, and to six months after the termination of the war as being equivalent to six months after the ratification of peace, seeing that six months would have been ample time to claim and take possession of the cotton, these considerations are of no avail whatever where the loan has no international status. But while it may be urged by those who take the by no means universally accepted view that neutrals may, with perfect legality, lend money to a belligerent independent State without being subsequently held liable by a conqueror to have their claims to repayment confiscated on the ground that they must have known their money was to be used in carrying on the war, the case is totally different where the loan is to rebels or to persons engaged in civil war against a State with international rights. The question may well be asked, Can private individuals lend money to populations in rebellion or engaged in civil war, and then claim that they did not know that the money was to be applied to purposes of rebellion? Can rebels, so long as the issue of the rebellion is still undecided, borrow for any other recognised purpose than that of rebellion?

It may be remarked also that there is a very wide difference between sales of war materials by a neutral to a belligerent independent State for cash or for some other property, the immediate delivery of which terminates the transaction, and similar sales made in exchange for bonds for future payment which must more or less depend for their value on the vicissitudes of war. So long as both belligerents are permitted to purchase war materials in any country for cash or other completed consideration, no assistance is really given, because an equivalent in value, and not merely the promise of an equivalent, is exchanged, and the seller may in fact have no knowledge whatever of the destination of the war materials. Having received full value he has no further concern in the matter. But it is doubtful if the giving of money to a belligerent independent State in exchange for bonds for future payment is not a material and deliberate assistance at a time when that State has no equivalent to give in cash or property, and whether, if one country was conquered by another, it would not be within the international right of the conqueror, in the case of loans contracted during the course of the war, to throw upon the holders of the bonds of such loans the onus of showing that the money advanced was not used in carrying on the war. The individual who deals for cash is free from all future consequences, because his transaction is completely closed; but is the individual who lends to a nation engaged in war, money on bonds for future payment, also free from future consequences? Is he not bound to look to the borrower and the borrower's probable future position, and when his borrower is defeated is he entitled to claim from the conqueror payment that the borrower himself could not claim if he had made the loans out of his private means? The case is totally different with debts contracted before war had begun, as the successful ruler *de facto* becomes a trustee for such debts; but does he also become a trustee for the repayment of money given by neutrals at a time when the borrower was carrying on a war in which he might be unsuccessful? Has the lender no responsibility, as a neutral lending to a belligerent, to assure himself that the money he expects to be repaid if the borrower be defeated is legitimately used for some peaceful purpose which in no way conflicts with his position as a neutral?

In the Confederate war due warning had been given that hostilities were being carried on between the United States and a large body of their own citizens, and the former had given the fullest notice that they were carrying on war, not for the conquest of an independent State, but for the recovery of a violated jurisdiction. Any assistance to the Confederates from neutrals was an international wrong to the United States, as helping to deprive them unjustly of their lawful jurisdiction. Having re-established their authority over the Southern States by the sacrifice of several hundreds of thousands of lives and several thousands of millions of dollars, it could hardly be expected that the United States would agree to repay to aliens the loans they subscribed to support this violation of United States jurisdiction; and, although doubtless many Southern people had to take the Dollar Bonds on compulsion, and therefore had, and still have an equitable claim to payment from the United States as having been innocent sufferers by the war, this is a ground of claim which cannot be urged on behalf of the holders of the Cotton Bonds.

The Cotton Bondholders assert a claim to the cotton which was hypothecated to them, of the greater part of which they allege they have been, and are, wrongfully deprived by the United States. They maintain that the loan was a purely commercial transaction, with the cotton lying within the Confederate States hypothecated to them as security; but it can hardly be claimed that the security was not dependent on the success of the Confederacy. For what are the facts? A usurping (as events proved) Confederacy by illegally (as events proved) exercising the powers of taxation and seizure within the lawful (as events proved) jurisdiction of the United States, acquires possession of large quantities of cotton, and being unable to export and sell it, owing to the blockade of the Southern ports, hypothecates in return for money this illegally acquired cotton to neutral aliens in foreign countries. It is important to observe that in consequence of the cotton being in the Confederate States and not in the independent custody of the lenders, the price at which it was hypothecated with the option to the lender of possessing himself of it, was 6d. per lb., at a time when it was worth in the open markets of the world, 1s. 6d. or 2s. per lb.; so that if this was a purely commercial transaction, it must be regarded as one with enormous prospective profit if it could have been fulfilled, and as showing beyond doubt that it was made under highly speculative conditions. After a time this cotton falls into the hands of the United States, and they seize and appropriate it as the property of the citizens of the United States from whom it had been illegally obtained by taxation or seizure, the United States being the lawful custodians of all property which the Confederate States had illegally acquired at the expense of the citizens of the United States.

It may be suggested further, that if it were possible to have all the circumstances of the acquisition and hypothecation of the cotton enquired into, it would not be surprising if holders of Dollar Bonds in the Southern States and Europe, came forward and claimed that the cotton was taken under physical and moral compulsion and Dollar Bonds given in return, and that the Dollar Bondholders had therefore a prior right to compensation for the cotton over the Sterling Cotton Bondholders.

It is hardly necessary to consider the allegation that the United States as conquerors were bound to take over the just obligations of the conquered Confederate States, because, as we have already shown, the United States only gained their former jurisdiction, while the Confederate States, having failed to assert their independence, and thus having been an illegal corporation, possessed nothing that could be conquered except what belonged to the United States themselves and to the legal State Governments of the South, of which the United States were the paramount guardians. The Confederate States had no just obligations except those that the United States might choose to respect, and when the latter refused to acknowledge the Cotton Bonds and the Dollar Bonds, and showed unmistakably that they would not permit any special legislation for the purpose of giving validity to these illegal Bonds, the latter were left without any authority legally responsible for them.

VI.—THE FOURTEENTH AMENDMENT.

The Fourteenth Amendment to the United States Constitution contains the following stipulation :—

"Neither the United States, nor any State, shall assume or pay any debt or obligation incurred in aid of insurrection or rebellion against the United States . . . . but all such debts shall be held illegal and void."

This is regarded by every authority quoted in the documents of the case of the Bondholders as the one great obstacle to the payment of the Confederate Debt. It is alleged by eminent jurists that this Amendment is unconstitutional, for the reason that it impairs the obligation of contracts which the Constitution as originally formulated expressly declares to be inviolable, and that it is void as being retrospective legislation in regard to contracts of which cognizance could be taken only by the Courts and not by the legislative power. To this the evident reply is, that the payments which this Amendment forbids are payments claimed on contracts which the United States Courts, or even the Courts of the reconstituted States of the South, could not fail to pronounce illegal on the ground of the illegality of the Confederacy and the objects of its existence. It is thus in no way retrospective legislation in restraint of any previously existing right or obligation; and from the time of the secession every act of the United States to recover their jurisdiction was a notice to all concerned, that every act in defiance or in deprivation of their authority was then in their eyes illegal, and would, if United States authority were re-established, be declared illegal by every tribunal in the United States.

The Fourteenth Amendment is in reality merely an emphatic record in few words of the actual bearing of then existing law, and except as authoritatively re-stating the law which might by many have been regarded as doubtful, it is altogether unnecessary, and is not the insurmountable obstacle to the Bondholders obtaining justice. The really insurmountable obstacle is that the payment of debts incurred by a rebellious people in endeavouring to set up within the national territory an independent State to the injury of the nation itself, is against public policy, because it would be an encouragement to rebellion and thus a danger to the security and integrity of every nation. So that the Fourteenth Amendment has not created any new disability, but the United States being a somewhat loosely organised Democracy with very extensive powers vested in the individual States, it was thought of the utmost importance at the close of the war to record in the most authoritative form known to the United States, namely, in the Constitution, the immemorial principle of public policy, that nations are bound to oppose and to discourage all attempts at rebellion against their own lawfully constituted authority, and that, therefore, the United States were bound to prohibit payment of all debts incurred in aid of the rebellion. This Amendment rendered it impossible for any State Legislature or State Court to attempt to deal illegally in any way with the Confederate Debt. And if public policy required the United States to refuse to pay debts incurred by the Confederate States, to the citizens of those States, much more does it require the United States to refuse payment of debts arising out of loans by neutral aliens to States in rebellion against the lawful authority of a Government in friendly relations with these neutrals.

It is always difficult in complicated cases to find suitable illustrations, and in all the cases cited in the documents referred to in illustration of the question of the Confederate Debt, not one seems to be a parallel case. But let us assume a case which will show, perhaps, more clearly than has been done, how little actual necessity there was for the Fourteenth Amendment or for *ex post facto* legislation, in order to render the payment of the Confederate Debt illegal. Let it be supposed that the inhabitants of the four provinces of Ireland were to withdraw from British jurisdiction, and to set up an independent Government; and if for the purpose of defending themselves against the blockade of their ports and other warlike operations to restore British jurisdiction, this usurping Government were to raise loans in the United States, they would be doing exactly what the Southern States and the Confederacy did in raising loans in Europe. All the municipalities of Ireland, and the local authorities in the counties would secede and form themselves into an Irish Republic just as the States seceded and formed a Confederacy. It will probably be rejoined that the States of the Union have much greater powers than are possessed by Irish provinces or municipalities, and it is true that they have greater legal powers; but they have no greater power to commit illegal acts against their supreme Government than the Irish municipalities have against the Government of the United Kingdom, and both of them having appealed to the " sacred right of insurrection," the illegal and unauthorised loans of the Irish Republic which, let it be assumed were made by Americans, could not be more illegal or more unauthorised than the illegal and unauthorised loans of the Confederate States. The defeat of the Confederate States decided that their debt was illegal, because United States jurisdiction was restored, and when the Irish Republic was once overthrown and British authority re-established, would Englishmen listen for a moment to the demands of American neutrals for the payment of the debt of the Irish Republic on the ground that Great Britain was the conqueror of the Irish Republic, and, as its successor, was bound to recognise and to pay all its just obligations? Yet Ireland has as valid a right to attempt to become a separate nation as the Confederate States had, if it desire to try to do such a thing. Would it be necessary for Great Britain to have *ex post facto* legislation in order to declare the debt of the Irish Republic to be illegal? It can hardly be thought that it would. The bonds of the Irish Republic would not be regarded as a legal claim for payment in any court of the British Islands, any more than the Confederate Bonds are accepted before United States tribunals. It is, therefore, public law and not the Fourteenth Amendment in itself, that stands in the way of the payment of the Confederate Debt.

But even if there had been retrospective legislation in regard to contracts which the fortune of war had rendered of doubtful validity, it must be admitted that at the close of a four years' conflict for their rights, and even for their existence, it was the duty of the United States to reconstruct the populations, lately in rebellion, into States, in such a manner and under such precautions as to ensure the completeness of their own jurisdiction, and as far as possible to discourage rebellion by every legitimate stipulation that might seem necessary to that end.

VII.—THE OPINIONS OF SIX CONTINENTAL JURISTS.

Dr. J. M. C. Asser, Professor Juris and Advocate in Amsterdam, and Dr. M. Th. Goudsmit, Doctor Juris and Advocate in Rotterdam, have given the following opinion :—

"So long, therefore, as the Confederation of the Southern States existed, the Loans constituted a legal debt, for which, after the dissolution of the Confederation, the States that had belonged to it must be deemed liable. The success of the Northern Armies and the re-establishment of the United States on their former basis, could not annihilate any liability legally contracted by or in the name of the Southern States. The United States Constitution of 1787 having respected the sovereignty of each State, and left to the States all the power not expressly delegated to the Confederation, their right of contracting loans cannot be contested, and loans authorised by a Congress to which the States had delegated that right are as valid as loans contracted by the States themselves, "*quod quis per alium fecit id ipse fecisse videtur.*"

"The Fourteenth Amendment to the Constitution of the United States quoted above, could not deprive the creditors of the Southern States of their claims upon these States. As far as this amendment concerns the special debts of any State, it must be considered as being of no legal force, because according to general principles of public law a confederation has not the right of annulling liabilities legally contracted by its members."

* * * * * * *

"It need not, however, be said that if the liability existed it could not be annulled by the debtor alone, so that Articles like those we refer to cannot be of any influence on the legal position of the creditors."

The above opinion does not sufficiently distinguish between the powers of the States so long as they are in the Union, and the powers of States or populations in rebellion against the Union. The authors of the opinion take no notice of the illegality, according to United States law, of secession, of forming State Governments and then a Confederacy, in defiance of the United States, with a view to becoming independent of the Union. But they say of States which had illegally seceded, that as the United States Constitution of 1787 left to the States all the power not expressly delegated to the United States Government, their right of contracting loans cannot be contested, and loans authorised by a Congress to which the States had delegated that right are as valid as loans contracted by the States themselves. It is impossible, however, thus to leap over the facts, as judged by United States law to which the verdict of the war relegated all questions as to the acts of the Confederacy and the States composing it, that the State Governments, the Confederacy, and all acts of the rebellion were illegal. If the Confederacy had succeeded in establishing its independence, then all acts of the Confederacy and the States would have been legal and the Dollar Bonds would have been a valid internal debt, while the Cotton Bonds would have been a valid international debt of the independent Confederate States. But they would have been valid debts, not in consequence of any power conferred upon the Southern States by the United States Constitution of 1787, but in virtue of the powers conferred by the Constitution of the Confederate States.

The following extracts are from the opinion of Dr. Achilles Renaud, Privy Counsel of the Grand Duchy of Baden, and Professor of Laws :—

"It has been maintained that as the loans in question were raised for an improper purpose, namely, for furthering and supporting the insurrection and rebellion of the Southern States against the *Union*,

[20201]

the Confederate States are not legally bound to pay the debts. Even if this be correct, it cannot in any way affect the legality of the loans, for the obligation of the recipient to return the value in a similar quantity and in like things, speaks for the validity of a loan or a contract, by which one person transfers a quantity of negotiable or valuable things to another, the said validity, it is true, depending upon the nature of the property, the consent of the parties, and the legal qualification of the taker and also the object of the loan."

* * * * * * *

"The motives which induced the contracting parties to make the contract is of no importance whatever from a legal point of view. If the Confederate States had raised the loans for the purpose of providing means for continuing the war against the Union, this would not have vitiated the legality of the loans. The same may be said of the assertion that the lenders in lending their money supported the said war."

* * * * * * *

"The assertion that the loans were raised for the improper purpose of supporting the rebellion, or were raised for or in the interest of the same, is the more unjustifiable, because, according to our foregoing observations, such an assertion could, in any case, only be available against the borrower, and not against the lenders of the loan; and if the prohibition of payment of the loans in question was made on the ground of the same having been raised by the usurping Authorities of Richmond, it is forgotten that the liabilities were contracted by an Authority which was recognised by the Southern States at the time the loans were contracted. In any case it is not the business of a debtor, if even the latter be a State, to declare that a certain private legal business, in which the said debtor contracts a liability, is null and void; but this must be left to the decision of the Courts of Law in the case of an action being instituted."

Dr. Renaud here lays down with considerable emphasis the principle that when loans are made, there is an imperative obligation on the part of the recipient of the money or property to repay the loans in terms of the contracts. In the case under consideration, the corporation formerly known as the Confederate States of America, effected certain loans by an authority residing exclusively in this corporation, and to this corporation the lenders undoubtedly looked for repayment. This corporation was and is bound to pay, these legal debts, so that no countenance is given to the view that "the Confederate States are not legally bound to pay the debts." But the usurping State Governments and the usurping Confederacy are totally distinct corporations from the present State Governments of the South, and it will hardly be maintained that the present State Governments are legally bound to pay debts which it would have been entirely beyond their legal power to have created, apart altogether from the consideration that the Confederacy was not only an illegal, but a rebellious corporation. The loans to the Confederate States were perfectly legal loans, and they would be perfectly legal and valid to-day if the Confederacy were in existence. But the United States were not the debtors to whom the Confederate Bondholders looked for payment, and in suppressing the rebellion and re-establishing their own former authority, they assumed none of the illegal obligations that the Confederacy had contracted in the attempt to form a separate Republic in violation of the rights of the United States.

Dr. Renaud does not sufficiently distinguish the very marked difference between loans made by neutrals to belligerent independent States and those made to belligerent rebellious Confederations. Even if neutrals might, according to international law, although it is very doubtful, make loans during war to both belligerents, which the conqueror if he annexed the whole country would be bound to respect in the case of the defeated borrower, it would still remain the fact that there is no international status in a loan made to rebels against a friendly Government, and therefore the creditor of the defeated rebellious Power can only appeal for payment to the national courts of the conqueror, and in these there can be no other decision than that the acts of the rebellious Power were illegal.

Dr. Renaud states that the allegation of the improper purpose for which the loans were raised could only be available against the borrower; but the borrower is no longer in existence, and it is manifest that the United States or the present State Governments had no concern either in the loans or their improper purpose. The legality of the loans is complete, but the borrower has ceased to exist, and has not left behind him any estate against which the holders of the loans can put forward their claims.

From the opinion of Dr. Jules Levita, Doctor of Law and Advocate of Paris, the following passages are cited:—

"The Congress of the Confederate States, after having obtained by its political and military organisation for the Southern States recognition as belligerent States, passed decrees authorizing the issue of loans. In decreeing these loans, pursuant to Section 8 of its Constitution, the Confederate Congress exercised, in the name of and with the concurrence of the thirteen States represented by it, the right incontestibly assured to each of them by the American Constitution of 1787 to contract public loans."

* * * * * * *

"It results from these clauses, which are not singular to the Constitutions of the States of the American Union (as the principle that the judges are independent of the legislative power is recognized by all free nations), that the Legislative Assemblies of the South had not the right to adjudicate upon a question of private property, and that the question of cancellation of a debt validly contracted, could only be decided by competent tribunals.

"These latter, in applying the principles upon which all rights of property and of claim rest, could not decree confiscation to the prejudice of the owner nor of the creditor. The Courts would have allowed, as provided by the Constitutions of the States, fair compensation to the holders of the bonds of the Confederate Debt."

* * * * * * *

"Their obligation is independent of the political changes which have been brought about. A country or a province conquered during a war, or pursuant to a treaty, is not discharged from its debts consequent upon the non-continuance of the Government which had contracted such debts."

Dr. Levita maintains that the Congress of the Confederate States in raising loans after their recognition as belligerents "exercised in the name of, and with the concurrence of the thirteen States represented by it, the right incontestibly assured to each of them by the American Constitution of 1787 to contract public loans." But the evident difficulty in accepting this view is that the Southern States usurped powers not granted to them by the Constitution of the United States, and violated fundamental laws by which they were bound, and having formed an illegal Confederacy hostile to the United States, which was recognised as a belligerent, neither the States nor the Confederacy could be said to be exercising powers granted by the Constitution of 1787, whilst they were deliberately violating that instrument. It can hardly be contended, when the States of the South had by violence become Confederate States, and had ceased by their own acts and declarations to be States of the United States, that they could legally exercise the powers of issuing loans in such a manner as to secure for such loans the authority and legality of loans issued by the States of the United States. The Confederate States had complete power of their own to raise loans for any purpose they might think fit, according, as Dr. Levita states, to Section 8 of the Confederate Constitution; and it was as a Sovereign Power that they issued their loans, for the legality of which they appealed to their authority under their own Constitution, and not under that of the United States.

As to the right of the Legislative Assemblies of the South to adjudicate upon private property, it is not necessary to offer any opinion; but in the similar case which has been supposed, that, namely, of the debts that might be contracted in the attempt to set up an Irish Republic, it is perfectly certain that it would be impossible for the bondholders of the Irish Republic to obtain a hearing in any Court of Ireland, or of any other part of the United Kingdom, and it is highly probable that the British Legislature would by retrospective legislation, affix pains and penalties to the acts and to the leaders of the Irish Republic.

The opinion of M. Lenté, Advocate of the Court of Appeal in Paris, and that of M. Henri Barboux, Batonnier of the Roll of Advocates in the Court of Appeal in Paris, both assume the correctness of the following statement, namely :—

That the Constitution of the American Union of 1787 concedes to each of the States of the Union power to contract public loans, and that consequently the Southern Confederated States assembled at Richmond had in principle the right to borrow individually in terms of that Constitution.

It need scarcely be repeated that the Confederate States were not States of the United States, nor were they exercising the powers of States of the Union, so that it is unnecessary to discuss the inferences they draw from premises which it is impossible to admit, as the subject has already been considered at length.

In a careful examination of the opinions of these six jurists, therefore, although they all take a favourable view as to the legality of the debt against the present States of the South, there do not appear to be any really valid grounds on which payment of the Confederate Debt could be legally demanded or enforced.

VIII.—CASES QUOTED IN FAVOUR OF THE CLAIMS OF THE BONDHOLDERS.

The case of the United States *v.* Prioleau and others, which was tried before Vice-Chancellor Page Wood (afterwards Lord Hatherley) in 1866, gives no support whatever to the case of the Bondholders. The cotton which the United States claimed as belonging to the Confederate States, and as having by the termination of the war become their property, had run the blockade and been brought to England, and thus it became subject to English Courts, which were bound to consider the claims of Prioleau, whose right of ownership or of lien for debt was decided to be valid by this neutral tribunal. Vice-Chancellor Wood held that the United States could only recover the cotton subject to the equities and liabilities attaching to it, one of which liabilities was the payment of a debt due from the Confederate States to Prioleau of £40,000.

But the cotton claimed by the Bondholders was not in England, nor under the cognizance of neutral courts, and as at the close of the war it fell into the possession of the United States, and was appropriated by them as property illegally acquired and held by a usurping Government, there were no equities attaching to it in favour of the Cotton Bondholders that could be enforced in any United States Court. The loan had no international character, and therefore had no claim to be considered anywhere but in the Courts of the United States.

The same objection as in the Prioleau Case exists in the case of the United States v. McRae, namely, that the equities that may be declared to be valid with regard to property in a neutral country, and before a neutral tribunal, may have no legal existence whatever in a belligerent country, and before courts which are bound to declare to be illegalities all acts done in aid of rebellion against their lawful authority. The United States declare that the cotton, which was hypothecated by a number of their rebellious citizens, was illegally acquired by the latter, and that the loan made upon the cotton by neutral aliens was without warrant in international law and thus could only be regarded as a gambling transaction. They assert, therefore, that claim to repayment cannot be brought before any court in the United States, nor can any equitable grounds be presented on which payment could reasonably be expected.

In the case that we have already supposed, of a rebellious attempt to set up an Irish Republic, the latter might levy taxes, and with the proceeds purchase flax or any other kind of property, and hypothecate this to the bondholders of their loan in the United States. But whether the Irish Republic lasted four months or four years after hostilities commenced, is it supposable, when British authority was finally re-established, that the British Government would hand over the hypothecated property that had fallen into their possession, to the holders of the bonds of the Irish Republic? This would be an exactly parallel case, and it is unnecessary to say that such a demand of the Irish bondholders would be rejected without much necessity for lengthened consideration.

There is a very marked distinction to be drawn between the legality of a loan raised by a belligerent in a neutral country, in so far as it does not infringe the laws to be observed by neutrals, and the responsibility of the other belligerent to repay the loan when he has defeated his rebellious citizens who applied the proceeds of the loan in endeavouring to deprive him of his own territory. The legality in a neutral country of the documents issued, is totally different from the legality of the loan as determined by the courts of the country in which the claim for repayment must be made.

"In 1842, Mr. Webster, on behalf of the United States Government, expressed himself . . . . . . as follows (the question being the international validity of loans to Texas, then in revolt from Mexico) :—'As to advances and loans . . . . made by individuals to the Government of Texas, or its citizens, the Mexico Government hardly needs to be informed that there is nothing unlawful in this, so long as Texas is at peace with the United States, and that these are things which no Government undertakes to restrain.' "—The Bondholders' Case, p. 33.

This is simply a question as to the right of neutrals to make loans to revolting States without infringing the laws of neutrality in their own country. But because Mexico as a belligerent, fighting to recover its own lawful authority, has no international right to call upon the United States to prohibit American citizens from aiding by loans the rebellious citizens of Mexico, can that be assumed to be a valid ground on which Mexico, if it had defeated the Texans, would have been bound to pay debts incurred by Texas in the unsuccessful effort to achieve independence? In the late draft of a proposed settlement (May, 1882) of the Mexican debt, the loans raised by Maximilian for the support of the Imperial cause were not recognised at all, and yet the case for their payment is very much stronger than that for the payment of the Cotton Bonds, having regard to the predominant position which Maximilian held for a time in Mexico.

"Mr. Holford's claim against the United States . . . . . . arising out of their annexation of Texas . . . . . . is in every respect similar to the present case of the Cotton Bondholders, except that no civil war preceded the claim in the case of the Texas loan. But, as regards seizure by the United States of the pledged property, the circumstances are identical. Mr. Hornby, the British Commissioner, said in the course of his argument, 'this clear and indisputable obligation of the United States has not only been thus duly acknowledged by the executive of the United States, but on three different occasions . . . . . . upon the express ground that the transfer of the right to levy imposts which Texas had, as a sovereign Republic, at the time of her annexation to the United States, and which antecedently she had appropriated expressly to the payment of this debt, bound the United States to do one of two things—either to pay the debt or surrender the pledge ; and not being able constitutionally to do the latter, it follows as a matter of irresistible consequence that she is both morally and legally bound to do the former.'"—The Bondholders' Case, p. 61.

The United States ultimately paid this claim. But the circumstances were very different from those of the Cotton Bondholders. It was not a province of the United States that had revolted and been defeated, it was an independent Republic, which became a State of the Union with the consent of its own citizens, and as the United States took possession of the sources of revenue that had been hypothecated for the payment of this debt, the obligation became an international one. It was in no way tainted with illegality, and was therefore acknowledged as valid on several occasions by the United States and ultimately paid.

"Now it is a received maxim of all warfare—foreign, and still more civil—that one belligerent State or party makes war against the other State or party, not against the individual citizens thereof, except so far as they may actually participate in the war, and so become amenable to its usages, and liable to its risks. The one State or party ought not, therefore, (analogously) to visit with pains and penalties, on the conclusion of the war,

[20201]

those individual citizens who have entered into financial relations with the only Government available for such purposes, and to whom that Government incurred debts. This, however, they would do by confiscating those debts. The Federal Courts have regarded the acts of the Governments of the revolted States as valid so far as those acts were unconnected with the rebellion. 'Texas v. White,' 7 Wallace, 170.

"Thus they have recognised the validity of a sale of land by a private citizen to the Confederate Government, see 'United States, Lyon et al, v. Huckabee,' 16 Wallace, 414.

"Contracts between citizens, payable in Confederate notes, were enforced, and the parties compelled to pay at the real value thereof, and not at the nominal value when payment was due. The notes were treated as a currency imposed by irresistible force."—The Bondholders' Case, pp. 56, 57.

This only shows that the United States recognised all contracts as valid that were entered into in the Confederate States during the rebellion, except those that were connected with the rebellion itself. That is, they recognised all those contracts made under Confederate rule that would have been valid if they had been made under United States rule, and refused to legislate so as to make legal all those acts that would have been illegal under United States rule, and amongst the latter the loans of the Confederacy.

The case of the Peruvian Bondholders is brought forward as showing that when Chili defeated Peru, it recognised the prior right of the Bondholders to the guano deposits that came under its political control, on the ground that the conqueror ought to take over and respect the just obligations of the conquered. It is alleged that in the same way the United States ought to have recognized the prior rights of the Cotton Bondholders in the cotton hypothecated by the Confederate States to the Bondholders. However, since the documents were issued in which the honourable course pursued by Chili at the outset is pointed out, the Government of that country has unfortunately shown a decided tendency to act towards the Bondholders in a manner utterly at variance with the most settled principles of international law. The cases, it will be seen, nevertheless, are not similar. Chili conquered a part of Peru to which, up till the time of conquest, Chili had no claim whatever; and, therefore, according to international law it was bound to respect the prior obligations of the independent State of Peru ; and as the guano deposits were hypothecated to the Bondholders, Chili was bound to respect the rights of the latter. It would be difficult, therefore, to find a stronger or more complete claim according to international law than that of the Peruvian Bondholders, seeing that they have a complete legal claim and a special hypothecation. On the other hand, the Confederacy never reached the status of an independent State, nor did the hypothecation of the cotton take place before the war, as in the case of Peru with the guano deposits. The United States did not conquer a new territory, it simply re-established its own former jurisdiction.

Then, again, it is alleged that if the Confederacy has been broken up, the individual States of which it was composed remain, and that as the partners in the Confederacy they are jointly and severally liable for the partnership debt. But as has already been stated, the Confederacy was an illegal corporation, and the State Governments that created it were illegal corporations, and as such they could not have legal successors. The present State Governments are new corporations created by law since the fall of the Confederacy, and therefore they have no liability for the illegal acts of the Confederacy or the States composing it. The only successors of the Confederacy and the States to be found, are the individual citizens of the Southern States who created the illegal State Governments and the illegal Confederacy, and although the Fourteenth Amendment prohibits the States from paying the Confederate Debt, it does not prohibit the citizens of the Southern States from doing so. They were the partners in the Confederacy, and are its legitimate successors, so far as it can be regarded as having any successors.

IX.—THE EQUITIES IN THE ORIGINAL CONTROVERSY BETWEEN NORTH AND SOUTH RESERVED.

In all that has been said regarding the Confederate Bonds as Confederate Debt, the object has been to examine if any legal or international grounds could be found on which a claim could be made either to the United States or to the Southern States for payment. But no such grounds have been found, so far as an examination of the materials under discussion has enabled a judgment to be formed.

This is far from implying, however, that all grounds for a claim are exhausted, because the discussion has been confined to the practical bearing of well known facts and of settled principles of international law, and has not touched upon the merits of certain equities that enter into the case, though they lie beyond the scope of the present examination. Nor is it meant to imply that there are equitable claims arising out of the fact that though the United States or the present State Governments are not the actual legal successors of the Confederacy, yet they are practically its successors, and therefore they ought to pay its debts. This is too weak and hopeless a basis on which to raise any expectation of payment on international grounds.

But there is some field for consideration by the United States in regard to the claims of the Dollar Bondholders in the "irrepressible conflict" between North and South which, it cannot possibly be doubted, led the Southern States to desire to protect slavery from the dangers to which their property in slaves was being subjected by the Northern Abolitionists, and which led them, in the hope of securing greater protection, to secede from the Union. The present discussion is not in any way concerned with the question as to the sacredness of the cause in which the Abolitionists were engaged, and besides most Europeans were strongly in favour of anti-slavery views. However objectionable the institution of slavery may have been in the eyes of Europeans and of Northern Abolitionists, it was nevertheless an institution under the protection of the law, while the attitude of the Northern Abolitionists—rightly or wrongly, is not in question—was hostile to slavery, and was hostile to the enforcement of the laws in regard to slaves. The British people had come face to face with the same question in the West Indian Islands, and they regarded the owners of slaves as having such complete legal rights in the ownership of their slaves, that in 1833 they voted out of the British Treasury £20,000,000 as compensation to the slaveholders in order that the slaves might be emancipated. The aim of the Northern Abolitionists was to free the slaves without compensation to the owners, on the ground that no man had a right to hold property in his fellowman, and this roused fierce antagonism in the South against the Abolitionists and Northern people generally. The fact that Northern statesmen should have spoken of the political relations between North and South as an "irrepressible conflict," shows that the nation was divided into two bitterly hostile sections, and it cannot be doubted that the South had very strong reasons for dreading that the power of the North, then in 1861 coming into complete ascendency in the National Government, would be a grave danger to the continuance of slavery, as it could hardly fail to take aggressive political action against that institution. The Fugitive Slave Law was a dead letter in all, or nearly all, of the Northern States, and finding the North so hostile to their special institution, they seceded in the belief that they would be peacefully allowed to form a Confederacy without interference by the United States; and doubtless also in the belief that, if interfered with, they would be able to maintain themselves against the power of the North.

Slavery, the evil legacy from past generations, and the bitter source of sectional hostility and hatred, has been abolished, and this menace to the peace, prosperity and unity of a great people, has ceased to be a national danger. In these circumstances, when the fierce conflict has been solved by a tremendous war, and there exists no longer any cause for dissension except the unfortunate remembrances and survivals of the war itself, the question of political expediency may now justly be held to be of supreme and paramount concern; and the original controversy between North and South may, with a view to the Northern people re-examining their own acts and their own attitude in the light of equity and political expediency, be summed up by saying, that, *the North was not altogether right, and the South was not altogether wrong.*

The war, as events happened, was inevitable, and its results are irrevocable, so that that is not a question to be considered. But there were misfortunes and injustices before it and incident to it, out of which arise important equities that a powerful and expanding nation, rich beyond the dreams of the generation that sustained the burden of the war, and capable of being united as they never have been before in their history, have the deepest interest in examining and satisfying. By so doing, they will not only perform a magnanimous act, not the least conspicuous among the great deeds recorded in the annals of the leading Commonwealths of the world, but they will cement together in the closest union the two great divisions of North and South, and in such bonds of strength and amity as, if achieved, would be beyond all price; while out of the mutual co-operation of the two formerly discordant sections, a gigantic inter-State commerce will arise, which will be a universal blessing to the whole American people. The time might then be looked forward to as not very remote, when the Fourteenth Amendment would be expunged from the Constitution as a symbol of a condition of strife and dissension which the entire people of the United States were anxious to forget, and which they desired should no longer disfigure the Charter of their Liberties.

X.—AN OMITTED CLAIM AGAINST THE UNITED STATES.

Whatever view may be taken of the legal or equitable claims of the Confederate Bondholders, there is a legitimate claim against the United States and the individual States of the South that has been omitted to be presented. When the war broke out between the North and the South the trade between Europe and the Southern States in cotton, sugar, tobacco, &c., on the one hand, and in European goods on the other, was one of very great dimensions, and there was in the South a very large amount of trade debts and of mortgages on property, owing to Europeans, besides a considerable quantity of property owned by Europeans which they were compelled to sell. A great part of these obligations, when realised, were remitted to Europe in the form of Dollar Bonds, that being the only available means of remittance from the Confederate States. The holders of these Bonds have always been in hopes that the time would come when they would be paid, and when, therefore, they would receive the value to which they were entitled. They knew that the Southern States were poor, that their State Bonds were for the time in default, and they thought that when the State debts were rearranged, the Dollar Bonds would also be provided for. That is the attitude of many Bondholders to-day. Thinking that, as they were not concerned in the war they had a valid security, they did not prefer their claims through their respective Governments to be presented at Washington at the same time that other claims arising out of the war were being settled.

Thus it comes that a large amount of debt which had no connection whatever with carrying on the war or with the Confederacy, remains unpaid by the Southern States to this day. That debt, it cannot be doubted, is a legal and valid claim against the United States no less than against the Southern States; and if the evidences of the debt are, under the compulsion of war, and by no choice of those to whom it is due, in their hands in the form of Dollar Bonds, there is no equitable ground on which payment of this debt can be refused. It must be particularly observed that although the Bonds held by those to whom these debts from the South were due, are Confederate Bonds, yet those who hold them, as representing Southern private debts or remittances, can rightfully claim that these Bonds so remitted are simply evidences of private legal debts that remain unpaid, and as such they can legitimately demand payment. The Confederate Debt is, according to United States law, illegal, but while this is so, it in no way affects the complete validity in the hands of neutrals, of a large portion of the certificates issued by the Confederacy in the form of Bonds, as undoubted evidences of private debts which had no connection whatever either with the war or the Confederacy, and which are simply accidentally connected with the name of the Confederate States in being represented by documents bearing their stamp, and which are illegal so far as the interest of the Confederate States is concerned, while they are perfectly legal so far as the interest of private neutrals is concerned, who received them under compulsion as representing legitimate private debts. These private debts, therefore, which it became impossible to settle in any regular manner on account of the war, and of which, in consequence of the remittance of these illegal Bonds and the general destruction of property and scattering of persons that the war entailed upon the South, it has been impossible to obtain any just settlement since the war, are a perfectly rightful claim as international debts against the United States as the Sovereign Power. Against the individual States of the South, they can only be regarded as private debts.

Now it is neither forbidden by the Constitution of the United States, nor by the Constitutions of the Southern States, nor by considerations of public policy, to pay such lawful debts as those to which we have referred as remaining unpaid. Not only are those debts unpaid, but the Europeans, to whom the evidences of the amount of these debts were remitted in Confederate Bonds, had to make large sacrifices in consequence of the diminution in all values resulting from the war, and had to be content with but a portion of the amount that they should have received if no hostilities had occurred. The amount to be paid in settlement of these debts, therefore, is a perfectly legitimate question for arbitration between the Governments of Great Britain, France and Holland on the one hand, as these are the countries chiefly interested, and the United States on the other hand.

It will probably be alleged that the Bonds were remitted in full payment of the debts, but that view cannot for a moment be sustained, because the jurisdiction of the United States was the only legitimate jurisdiction within the territory of the Republic in the eyes of neutral aliens, and neither the United States nor the legal State Governments of the South could possibly hold that the Confederate Bonds were a legal payment of private debts to absent neutral aliens, while they declared by provisions in the Constitutions of the United States and the Southern States that the Confederate Debt was illegal, and should never be paid by the United States or by any of the States. The Bonds thus remitted were, therefore, not a payment at all, but simply so far as United States law is concerned, evidences of debt due but not paid, a recognition that citizens of the South owed certain amounts of money to their European creditors, and they are to-day evidences of these unpaid debts. But besides the private debts owing from Southern citizens to Europeans, the evidences of which are to be found among the Confederate Bonds, there are also in these Bonds equally valid debts due to many loyal Southern citizens and to Europeans who had to take Confederate Bonds by compulsion in exchange for property with which they were forced to part to the Confederate authorities, and are thus innocent holders of such Bonds in not having had any part in carrying on the war. And these debts also the United States are entitled to pay, partly on equitable and partly on international grounds. It is highly probable that a large quantity of the cotton hypothecated to the Cotton Bondholders, which fell into the hands of the United States, was forcibly acquired in exchange for Dollar Bonds, and thus innocent holders of such Bonds have been unjustly deprived of their property and its value, both by the Confederacy and by the United States. Thus it will be seen that a candid examination of the facts by the United States authorities could hardly fail to lead to a recognition by them of a large amount of genuine claims, partly due to Europeans for private Southern debts and for property taken by force, and partly to innocent Southern citizens, all represented in the Confederate Bonds, but in no way coming in conflict with the Fourteenth Amendment, or with any considerations of public policy. And though the private debts owing to Europeans were debts of Southern citizens, yet the claim to repayment is one which is so clearly valid in international law, that the United States cannot refuse to examine and to pay them.

The Southern States cannot dispute the fact that in the complete paralysis of trade with Europe during the rebellion, immense losses were sustained by European merchants and capitalists, who had an enormous trade pending when the war broke out, were under large advances to planters and others, and were extensively interested in property in the South, most of the proceeds of the wreck of which, was exported to Europe in the form of Confederate Bonds in the absence of any other form of remittance. It is of the utmost importance to the credit of the Southern States, not to its name merely, but what is of infinitely more importance, to its borrowing power, that these claims, and all the State debts, should be put on some settled footing. The States of the South cannot raise money in Europe for the construction of railways or for other enterprises except at exorbitant rates, and it is most important in their own interest that their credit should approximate more closely to the exceptionally high credit that the Northern States enjoy, and it may not be found to be outside the duty of the latter to help the South in arriving at a consummation so desirable.

It is important to remark, that it would be not only an act of wisdom, but that it is an act of duty on the part of the United States to deal in a liberal spirit with the legitimate claims of the loyal citizens of the Southern States. Not to act thus is to encourage rebellion, because it will be to give an impressive warning that as soon as hostilities commence, it will be better for persons who might incline to be loyal or at least passive to throw themselves heart and soul into the rebellion, as loyalty will bring loss and ruin if the rebellion be suppressed owing to the conqueror treating loyal and rebel alike, whereas the hearty co-operation of rebels and those inclined to be loyal might cause the rebellion to be successful, in which event those who had lost their property in the cause of the rebellion would obtain compensation. Thus it is the duty of the United States, as a matter of public policy, to pay the legitimate claims of Southern loyal citizens for property taken by force in exchange for Dollar Bonds, to the amount that such debts may be fairly estimated to be represented in the Dollar Bonds.

When the United States shall have agreed upon the amount of these debts that they are prepared to pay, then it might seem that a difficulty would arise as to what special Bonds represent these debts, as there is no register by which they can be identified. But there need not be any great amount of trouble in settling matters. It must be remembered that the British Government paid the Alabama Award without any special statement of the exact claims to the payment of which the money was to be devoted. In the Alabama Award the amount of the damage was estimated by arbitrators and paid, and the British Government left to the United States Government the responsibility of extinguishing all the claims arising out of the Alabama's acts. In the same way, the British, French and Dutch Governments might take the amount of the Award for the payment of these private debts that are represented by Confederate Bonds, and might undertake to extinguish all the claims arising out of them. Or it might be simpler and more satisfactory for the United States Government to treat directly with the Bondholders, so as to extinguish all the lawful claims of the holders of Dollar Bonds. In whatever way, however, the amount of the Award may be distributed, that will not in any manner alter the amount of the debts that may be declared to be due, which is the sole question to be considered by the United States and the States of the South. It will be recollected that a policy similar to this was followed by the United States at the close of their War of Independence, when, owing to the very great difficulties attending the recovery of debts between citizens of the United States and of Great Britain, that had accrued owing to transactions before or unconnected with the war, the United States paid to Great Britain a lump sum in liquidation of these private claims of Englishmen against Americans, and left it to the British Government to extinguish all the claims of their citizens. Much more valid are the claims of neutrals, who, by receiving for debts due and for sales of property mere evidences of indebtedness by Southern citizens, and mere certificates of the value of property forcibly taken by the Confederacy, have thus suffered as much as if they had not merely been belligerents, but as if they had been rebels.

The amount of the Award being available in the hands of the United States Government, or being paid over to the European Governments the only practicable method of adjustment will be, in the absence of complete proof of the special Bonds on which the whole amount of the Award ought to be paid, to distribute this amount over all the Dollar Bonds that are presented within a certain time, and then all these Dollar Bonds, thus cancelled, can be delivered to the United States Government. If there be anything unsatisfactory in this method of proceeding, it will at least be no injustice to the United States, because they will only pay their lawful debt, though there may be unavoidable injustice to loyal Southern citizens, and to those European creditors of Southern citizens, who, by their own thoughtlessness and carelessness, neglected the opportunity at the proper time of presenting their claims to their respective Governments to be brought before the Commissions that sat at Washington for the settlement of such claims. But there is no other way in which these debts of European and Southern citizens can be extinguished than by cancelling all the Dollar Bonds that may be presented, as when that is done there will be no possible doubt that all the evidences of these private Southern debts and of the legitimate claims of Southern citizens shall have been given up, and the debts and claims thus extinguished; even if a less sum shall have been paid on some Bonds than might have been if the Bonds had been specially marked, and if payment shall have been made on other Bonds which, if they could have been distinguished, would not have received any payment at all.

This is a perfectly valid international claim on behalf of Europeans, which the British, French and Dutch Governments, whose citizens are

[20201]

chiefly interested, can without hesitation present to the Government of the United States, and which the United States, after satisfying themselves by arbitration or otherwise as to the amount, may confidently be expected to pay. The claim on behalf of loyal Southern citizens, to repayment for property represented also in the Dollar Bonds, is one the validity of which the United States cannot in justice refuse to recognise.

LONDON, *February 1st*, 1884.

www.ingramcontent.com/pod-product-compliance
Lightning Source LLC
Chambersburg PA
CBHW030710110426
42739CB00031B/1633